# HOLD THE FLAG HIGH

Catherine Clinton

Illustrated by Shane W. Evans

KATHERINE TEGEN BOOKS
*An Imprint of HarperCollinsPublishers*

Amistad

FOR JAMES M. MCPHERSON
—C.C.

THANK YOU, GOD, DEDICATED TO MY FAMILY
—S.E.

Hold the Flag High
Text copyright © 2005 by Catherine Clinton
Illustrations copyright © 2005 by Shane W. Evans
Manufactured in China. All rights reserved.
www.harperchildrens.com

Library of Congress Cataloging-in-Publication Data
Clinton, Catherine, date.
  Hold the flag high / Catherine Clinton ; illustrated by Shane W. Evans—1st ed.
    p. cm.
Summary: Describes the Civil War battle of Morris Island, South Carolina, during which Sergeant William H. Carney became the first African American to earn a Congressional Medal of Honor by preserving the flag.
  ISBN 0-06-050428-5 ~ ISBN 0-06-050429-3 (lib. bdg.)
  1. Morris Island, Battle of, S.C., 1863 (July 10-September 7)—Juvenile literature. 2. Carney, William H., 1840-1908—Juvenile literature. 3. African American soldiers—Massachusetts—Biography—Juvenile literature. 4. United States. Army. Massachusetts Infantry Regiment, 54th (1863-1865)—Juvenile literature. 5. United States—History—Civil War, 1861-1865—Participation, African American—Juvenile literature. [1. Morris Island, Battle of, S.C., 1863 (July 10-September 7) 2. Carney, William H., 1840-1908. 3. United States. Army. Massachusetts Infantry Regiment, 54th (1863-1865). 4. United States—History—Civil War, 1861-1865—Participation, African American. 5. Fort Wagner (S.C.)] I. Evans, Shane, ill. II. Title.
  E475.63. C55 2005                                          2003011956
  973.7'34—dc22

Typography by Jeanne L. Hogle
1  2  3  4  5  6  7  8  9  10
❖
First Edition

When the American Civil War broke out in 1861, the North and South had been quarreling for decades over the future direction of the country. The southern states wanted to create a new nation, a confederacy, independent of the United States. The federal government sought to put down the rebellion and restore the country as one Union.

After the Emancipation Proclamation freed the slaves in January 1863, African American soldiers joined the Union army and the fight to end slavery. The battle of Fort Wagner in July 1863 was one of the first occasions when black troops were sent into combat. . . .

The only thing scarier than a battle is the night before a battle. While soldiers swapped stories and took out pictures of their sweethearts and children, Sergeant William H. Carney strolled among the campfires.

A homesick private played his harmonica sweet and low. Carney draped a blanket around the shoulders of Company C's drummer boy, a young slave who had run off from his master to join the fight. Carney assured him, "Tomorrow's gonna be a big day for us, Ned. You'll be drumming us to glory."

Carney was one of the few black officers in the Massachusetts Fifty-fourth, a new African American regiment formed in the spring of 1863.

Carney's men took pride in the shiny brass buttons on their uniforms and new rifles on their shoulders. Just a few weeks before, they had paraded through the streets of Boston. Ladies had waved handkerchiefs, and all had shouted hurrahs and farewells. Then the Fifty-fourth Regiment had set sail to fight in far-off South Carolina.

Once they arrived, the soldiers set up camp south of
Charleston Bay. Their first battle would come tomorrow.
This was the day they had all been waiting for, the
soldiers told themselves as they headed off to sleep.
Carney kicked out the fire. An owl hooted in the
distance. Ned, the drummer boy, wondered if it was really
an owl. Maybe it was the signal of a Confederate spy.

Sarge, I don't know what it'll be like when the Rebs start shootin'. I'm feeling scared—and—and—" he stuttered, "and what if I get lost?"

"Son, you just play that drum, and remember what we're fighting for. Old Glory will lead the way."

"Old Glory?" Ned asked.

"Sure, son, keep your eyes on the flag," said Carney. "Like hundreds before us and thousands after, just follow those Stars and Stripes, and you can't go wrong."

"I can't go wrong," Ned murmured as Carney tucked him into his bedroll.

Then the sergeant said a little prayer, hoping it would be true.

Long before the sun rose, the men of the Fifty-fourth awoke to prepare for battle. They checked and rechecked their rifles, making sure flints were dry and bayonets sharp and shined. Ned worked hard, filling canteens with water.

After a breakfast of hardtack and coffee, each soldier had his name pinned onto the back of his uniform. This way, soldiers who did not survive the battle could be identified. Soldiers who could write helped those who couldn't.

Carney tipped his hat at the color-bearer. He was the soldier who carried the regiment's flag into battle on a short flagpole, called a staff. "We're all counting on you, brother."

The wind whipped the banner, held aloft on its staff: back and forth; then again, back and forth. Soldiers bristled with anticipation.

Ned could see their commanding officer, Robert Gould Shaw, approaching on horseback. As he galloped up, spurs gleaming on his heels and a fringed silk sash across his chest, the colonel seemed to own the day.

But when Shaw dismounted, Ned noticed that his pale face was nearly as white as his stallion. Ned wondered, *Could he be scared, too?*

Maybe Shaw *was* a bit afraid; he had already been wounded in battle once. But his speech to his troops betrayed no fears. Shaw fired up his men for battle. The Fifty-fourth had been picked to lead the charge against Fort Wagner—the Confederate outpost guarding Charleston. Chests swollen with pride, these soldiers could hardly wait. They would gladly follow Shaw to the ends of the earth, eager to prove their courage under fire.

The artillery shelled all day, but finally the generals were ready to send in the infantry. "Forward, march!" the order rang out.

An endless line of men in blue snaked along the sand. They headed for the fortress towering on the horizon.

Ned solemnly drummed out the beat—footfalls and drumsticks in syncopation. He glanced at the flag snapping in the stiff breeze. The gulls gently swooped, as waves lapped the shore. . . .

In a split second, everything tilted. Cannonballs pounded the ground. Bullets pelted helter-skelter. A greenish-yellow glow of smoke rose at the same time bodies began to fall. Streams of blood flowed into the foam, washing out to sea. The metallic taste in Carney's mouth mixed with the fear rising in his throat.

Ned could barely hear the drum over the roar.

Then a shell exploded behind him, and he fell to his knees.

His heartbeat pounded in his ears as he tried to get his bearings. Uninjured but dazed, Ned scanned the horizon.

Far above, he could see Colonel Shaw lit by the firelight from exploding shells. He was mounting a rampart, saber in hand, shouting: "Forward, Fifty-fourth," as he disappeared into the breach. But where was the flag?

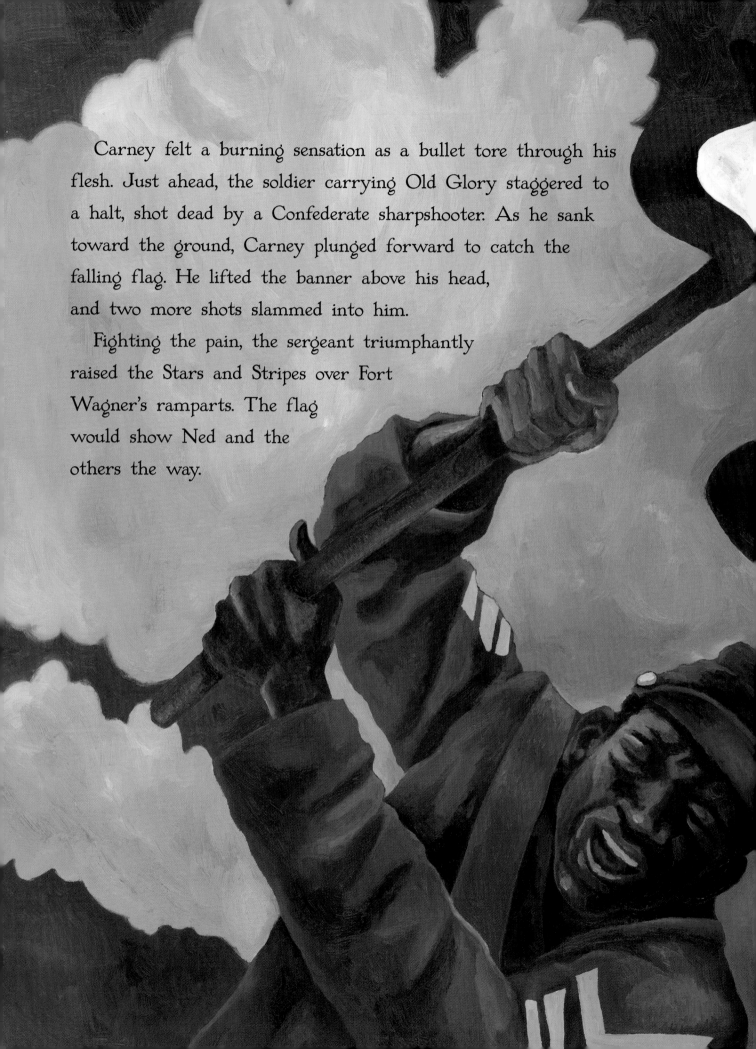

Carney felt a burning sensation as a bullet tore through his flesh. Just ahead, the soldier carrying Old Glory staggered to a halt, shot dead by a Confederate sharpshooter. As he sank toward the ground, Carney plunged forward to catch the falling flag. He lifted the banner above his head, and two more shots slammed into him.

Fighting the pain, the sergeant triumphantly raised the Stars and Stripes over Fort Wagner's ramparts. The flag would show Ned and the others the way.

Many hours later, when the Union bugler finally sounded
retreat, the federal soldiers straggled away from the fort,
defeated. Yet Carney carried the flag safely back behind
Union lines before he collapsed. Ned and other members of
the Fifty-fourth Regiment surrounded their wounded sergeant's
cot. They congratulated him as Carney murmured,
"The old flag never touched the ground."
Those who survived the battle of Fort
Wagner would never forget their brave
Sergeant Carney, who showed the
way by holding the flag high.

# EPILOGUE

Confederate troops held their position and declared victory at Fort Wagner on July 19, 1863. However, the Massachusetts Fifty-fourth Regiment took great pride in their performance, tested in battle.

Long after the Civil War had ended, Sergeant Carney appeared in Boston in 1897 at an unveiling ceremony. A monument for Colonel Robert Gould Shaw, who lost his life at Fort Wagner, was being dedicated. Carney and other members of the Fifty-fourth had contributed funds to erect an impressive bronze memorial honoring their fallen leader. At this solemn occasion, Carney received a standing ovation. His courageous act to preserve the flag was a tribute to those who died to defend it.

William H. Carney was eventually awarded the Congressional Medal of Honor—the first African American to earn this tribute.

# TIME LINE

**FEBRUARY 29, 1840**   William Carney was born a slave in Virginia.

**1850s**   Carney is purchased, emancipated, and reunited with his father, who escaped to New Bedford, Massachusetts, on the Underground Railroad.

**APRIL 12, 1861**   Confederates fire on Fort Sumter in Charleston, South Carolina; the Civil War begins.

**JANUARY 1, 1863**   President Lincoln issues the Emancipation Proclamation.

**FEBRUARY 1863**   William Carney enlists in one of the newly organized colored regiments, the Massachusetts Fifty-fourth.

**MAY 28, 1863**   The Massachusetts Fifty-fourth Regiment, led by Colonel Robert Gould Shaw, sets sail from Boston, to fight in South Carolina.

**JULY 18, 1863**   Battle of Fort Wagner outside Charleston, South Carolina

**FEBRUARY 1865**   The men of the Massachusetts Fifty-fourth march victorious into Charleston.

**APRIL 9, 1865**   Confederate General Robert E. Lee surrenders to General Ulysses S. Grant at Appomattox Court House, in Virginia; the Civil War ends.

**MEMORIAL DAY, MAY 1897**   Dedication of the Shaw Memorial, Boston, Massachusetts

**MAY 23, 1900**   Congress issues a citation awarding William Carney the Medal of Honor in recognition of his valor at the Battle of Fort Wagner.

**DECEMBER 8, 1908**   William Carney dies at the age of sixty-eight.

## RECOMMENDED RESOURCES

### WEBSITES

memory.loc.gov/ammem

www.nga.gov/feature/shaw

www.nps.gov/boaf/54th2.htm

### BOOKS

Clinton, Catherine. *The Black Soldier: 1492 to the Present.* Boston: Houghton-Mifflin, 2000.

McPherson, James. *Marching Toward Freedom: Blacks in the Civil War, 1861-1865.* New York: Facts on File, 1991.

Mettger, Zak. *Till Victory Is Won: Black Soldiers in the Civil War.* New York: Lodestar Books, 1994.

### FILM

*Glory,* directed by Edward Zwick, 1989.